Ac[...]

A Pocket Gu[...] [...]

Don't just read this useful little book. Take time to "do the work," remembering it's your effort that will make the difference. Do the processes, do them again, and make them part of your life. Good change will come when you take up your own cause for a happier life.

—Joy Aiken, Author

As a psychotherapist, this book brought up thoughts of the wounded healer archetype with its desire to help others heal. The concise and clearly stated descriptions are full of information intended for anyone to read and understand in the quest for self-love. A love of mystery and heartfelt encouragement for the reader are prominent in each chapter. The processes are practical, helpful, and useful. You will find healing along the path to self-love.

—Dr. Kianna Zielesch Ph.D., Psychologist
Code 3 Mind Health, Inc.

A Pocket Guide to Self-Love

Simple Steps to Love Yourself More

Lesley Epperson

A Pocket Guide to Self-Love
Simple Steps to Love Yourself More
Copyright © 2024 by Patricia Lesley Epperson

Lesley Epperson
Joyfriends Tiny Press
PO Box 2294 Fort Bragg, CA 95437
512 909-2970
lesleyepperson@gmail.com
www.lesleyepperson.com

Publisher's Cataloging-in-Publication
(Provided by Cassidy Cataloguing Services, Inc.)

Names: Epperson, Lesley, author.
Title: A pocket guide to self-love : simple steps to love yourself more
    / Lesley Epperson.
Description: : First edition. | Fort Bragg, CA : Joyfriends Tiny Press, [2024]
Identifiers: ISBN: 979-8-9903467-0-3 (paperback) | 979-8-9903467-1-0
        (ebook) | LCCN: 2024910240
Subjects: LCSH: Self-esteem. | Self-acceptance. | Love. | Affirmations. |
    Introspection. | Diaries-- Authorship. | LCGFT: Self-help
    publications. | BISAC: SELF-HELP / Personal Growth / Self-
    Esteem.
Classification: LCC: BF697.5.S46 E66 2024 | DDC: 158.1--dc23

Book Production by Cypress House
Cover Design by Allegra Pescatore

Printed in the USA

2 4 6 8 9 7 5 3 1

First edition

Dedication

I dedicate this book to Dr. Deborah King. For twenty-two years, Dr. King's kindness and patience led me past fear and anger. She allowed me to find my way out of darkness. She didn't push when I was stressed. She protected me from myself and others. I will never forget her.

Dr. King, I wish you a long and exquisitely happy retirement. I'm eternally grateful for your gentle guidance through more than two decades of constant change. You were my rock. Now I am your Healing Warrior.

Gratitude

I thank Sage Grey for reading, editing, and providing suggestions for making this book better. I'm immensely grateful to her for being there as it went from three chapters to a completed manuscript. Sage provided feedback that made this guide more valuable in many ways.

I'm also grateful for my dog extraordinaire, Khanju, who somehow found patience and understanding as I wrote instead of taking him for long walks along the coastal trail. The walks we did take were special, as we sat watching the ocean waves and the whale migration.

A Pocket Guide to Self-Love is more than an overview of the desire for and nature of self-love. Packed with information, the book offers practical and concise ways to be happier and kinder to yourself and others when life feels chaotic. Chapters include processes to guide you through healing emotional blocks, why words you use are important, and developing appreciation for the unique person you have always been. Skip any processes you aren't ready for and return to them later. The only rule is to tell yourself how much you love yourself every day.

This little book can be referenced and re-read as often as you like. No matter where you are right now, nothing can stand in the way of you loving you. Remember, it is always a good time to love yourself more.

Table of Contents

Introduction

In early November 2020, I followed the nudge of my soul and dove deep inside myself. I planned to be immersed in meditation and healing for two months. It would be *eight months later*—June 2021—before I emerged from this self-imposed isolation. I felt like a completely different person, amazed at how much I had changed. I actually loved myself for the first time I could remember.

During that time, I used meditation, visualization, emotional clearing, shadow work, forgiveness, and inner-child healing, as well as techniques to release through movement, including yoga and dance. I dealt with whatever arose at the time. I kept lists of emotions and fears at the root of my emotions, beliefs and feelings deeply bound together, ways to heal, and ways to let go. None of it was easy.

When I started this journey, I did not love myself. I never once believed I could love my whole self. I had a great deal of self-loathing for who I was. While I put up sticky notes all over my home and wrote *Hola, bella* (*Hi, beautiful*) in red lipstick on the bathroom mirror, I could not look at myself and say, "I love you." I accepted that I might never experience self-love, no matter how essential it is to giving and receiving love.

It was April 2021 before the tickle of angel wings filled my heart with love for who I was becoming, who I had always been. The day I first experienced the stirrings of self-love was light and happy, as I said over and over how much I loved who I was, flaws and quirks and all. It was the first time I actually believed I could rise above life's struggles and heal. I continue to feel emotions I was unable to express as a child come forward for release. I discover more about myself every day. I want to be strong, confident, and whole. I feel joy for the first time in years.

I started this book to be an uncomplicated guide for anyone who wants to love themselves or love themselves more. There is no one way to develop self-love, and many avenues arrive at the same destination. I've included some of the processes I used to discover who I was and who I wanted to be.

I tried to put this guide in logical order, with related processes and books I found useful. For me, it was important to choose my own path. Only after I worked with what came up in meditation each day did I feel prepared to take a deeper dive. The books listed in the resources section offer more detailed information than I present here. You might become overwhelmed if you start with them, so I suggest that you begin with this guide and expand when you feel ready.

I also recommend using the processes you feel drawn to, though the first two are essential. Tell yourself "I love you" every day. Tell yourself "I love you more" every day. Put your hand on your heart and tell yourself all the things you need to hear. This is the foundation for the rest of the journey.

Spend as much or as little time as you need on each chapter. If you're not ready, skip a chapter or process. I did emotional clearing last, and continue to work on clearing suppressed emotions. While each chapter builds on the prior one, listen to your heart. Don't force yourself to do anything that makes you uncomfortable. You know better than anyone what you can manage. Honor that.

Journal freely, without judgment, in whatever form you feel drawn to. I keep a journal called *I Just Realized....* It's filled with realizations that have had a significant impact on me. Pick up a nice solid journal and simply start writing down thoughts. Your authentic voice will emerge from the pages. It's a valuable way to see how far you've come.

I have continued to use many of the processes in daily life. Reviewing the chapters and processes will help you strengthen the foundations you've built. You may notice concepts that you didn't catch the first time. I leave it up to the reader to find their own path. Discover what works and what doesn't for you. When you are ready, dive deeper into any subject by checking out the resources listed at the end of this guide. You can't get this wrong.

1

Loving Who You Are

Loving yourself is a mysterious and magical path to a happy life.
—Lesley Epperson

Self-love is foundational for happiness. You can only fully love someone else if you love yourself first. You can't love yourself from a place of the ego, which will remind you of all the reasons you shouldn't love you. Move from your mind to your heart. Your heart knows the truth.

Let go of everything you've told yourself about who you are. Forget all that others have said about you. Self-love comes from a place of acceptance of who you really are, not the person who family members, friends, partners, teachers, bosses, society, and even you believe you are. Forget the old stories—it's time to write a new one.

Who are you? You're more than you ever imagined. You transcend the flesh, bones, organs, age, mind, emotions, occupation, and hobbies that make up the physical form and personality of being human. **You are love. And you are infinitely lovable.**

Process 1: Tell Yourself "I Love You" Every Day

Put your hand on your heart and say, "I love you, <your name>."
  Repeat at least three to five times a day for two weeks.
  For best results repeat many times every day.

Process 2: Think of A Beloved Family Member, Close Friend, Child, or Pet

Notice the quality of the love you have for them and how it feels in your heart. Hold this feeling as you repeat Process 1.

Do this as often as you can, transferring the love you feel for your loved one into a feeling of love for yourself.

2

You Are Unique

To accept oneself completely is to know the truest kind of self-love.
—Anonymous

To fully love who you are, you need to love more than your good qualities. You need to love all of you, including the parts you've hidden from yourself and others—also known as *shadow*—as well as your unique gifts and talents.

Talents are areas you're naturally skilled in, such as writing, networking, managing people, mechanical repairs, and the like. You are uniquely suited to use your talents across many areas of life.

Gifts are unique skills that you may or may not be aware of. We all have gifts to share with the world. Gifts can be something you discover by accident or by necessity. They differ from talents in that they're more like gems that appear when you face challenges. They include empathy, intuition, compassion, strength, courage, and wisdom. While gifts are part of our shared human experience, it's the combination of gifts that makes you unique.

Shadow Aspects can be difficult to find on your own, but you'll see them reflected in your relationships and reactions. When a friend reacts to something you say, it's like looking into a mirror. You don't see yourself as they see you, and this is a clue that they're seeing what you've kept hidden. This reflection can uncover what parts you hid as a child to stay safe, as an adult trying to fit in, or as a person with unresolved drama.

Repeating patterns in your life can also point to hidden shadow aspects as they come up for healing. In loving your whole self, the shadow invites you to discover, welcome, accept, and integrate parts of yourself that are not easy to embrace. Only when you accept what's hidden within can you let go. This is essential to growth as a human and a soul, as you learn to respond rather than react. Shadow also contains gifts and talents you have yet to discover.

The combination of your talents, gifts, and shadow aspects makes up the unique version of who you are and who you can be.

Process 3: Explore Your Talents, Gifts, and Shadow Aspects

Create an inventory of your talents, gifts, and shadow aspects. Under each heading, list at least five talents, gifts, and shadow aspects you've discovered. Ideally, sit in silence and let the information come to you.

Start with your talents and gifts, which will give you additional ways to see and appreciate who you are. The shadow aspects will serve as a guide to what you've uncovered, as repressed parts of you come up to be acknowledged and healed. In addition, shadow can reveal hidden talents and gifts waiting to be discovered and explored.

3

Embrace Your Emotions

When I let go of what I am, I become what I might be.
—Lao Tzu

To accept that you experience a wide range of emotions is to fully embrace your whole self. To experience emotions is an authentic expression of being human. We hide behind a mask of group identity, many of us never allowing ourselves to be individuals. What you're feeling is held hostage by a mind that learned speaking your truth comes with a price.

As children we learn that some emotions are good and others are bad. As a child you began to repress feelings that your family deemed unacceptable. As you grew up, you found additional emotions that didn't conform with society's rules, and suppressed those as well. It's no wonder few adults can say why they're unable to express how they truly feel.

Emotions you reject will continue to arise until they're healed. To learn to express emotions in healthy ways, you need to accept that you have a range of emotions you haven't been able to fully express and let go of your attachment to them.

In the following processes, you'll become aware of and welcome emotions you haven't been able to fully express and release attachment to them. To embrace your emotions, be mindful of what comes up for you. You can accomplish this during meditation, or in the midst of conflict, by recognizing what you're reacting to and understanding why.

Process 4: Awareness of Emotions

Spend a day or two listing all your emotions as they arise. You'll be surprised by the range of both positive and negative emotions you go through every day. Highlight any emotions you feel with unusual intensity.

Note where in your body you feel each specific emotion. Place your hand over the part of your body where the feeling is most intense and say, "Love to you." Your touch will calm any discomfort as you prepare to welcome your emotions to be seen, heard, integrated, transformed, and released.

Process 5: Welcome the Emotion

Sit quietly and breathe. You may find that an emotion comes up on its own. If it does, work with that one. Alternatively, you can use the emotion you felt most intensely when you did Process 4.

Address the emotion by name as you welcome it. For example, you could say, "Hello, Anger." Ask if there's anything it wants to tell you. Listen. Take note of any random thoughts that arise. Be curious. You want to fully experience the emotion.

Human emotions are complex. Though it will be uncomfortable as the feeling flows through your body, express gratitude for how it helped you cope as a child. You could say something like "Thank you for being there to make me feel safe when I needed you most."

Notice all the feelings surrounding the emotion. Feel these feelings fully. Have compassion for yourself and others. Forgive yourself for any times you used emotions in unhealthy ways. Bring yourself back to the body and notice any changes in where you feel the emotion. A full-body shake can help the nervous system adapt to these changes. Shake it off.

Write down the emotion in a journal or notebook. List any feelings that accompany the emotion, and all the ways they make you uncomfortable. You might want to list healthier ways to express your feelings, or note any thoughts that come up when you work with the emotion. It's common to address stronger emotions, such as anger and grief, more than once. Refer to the list you created in Process 4 to keep track of which emotions you've worked with. You may also want to give context around the part of the emotion that moved through your body, especially if it was a specific situation. For instance, if your anger felt like it was in response to abandonment or rejection, note that.

Process 6: Letting Go

Sit quietly and take a few deep breaths. Let the exhale be longer than the inhale until you feel fully relaxed. Be present in the moment with no expectations. When a thought or emotion comes up, watch it move through you and disappear.

Do not identify with the emotion that arises, pleasant or not. Imagine you are the ocean, with waves that rise and fall. Note the waves of feelings that accompany the emotion. Know that what you feel does not define you.

Do this for as long as you need to, witnessing the ebb and flow of your thoughts, emotions, and feelings. Once the intensity of the emotional release subsides, continue to let the emotion flow through you.

To complete the process, stretch and come back fully into your body. Expect the emotion to continue to release as you go on with your day. Drink lots of water. Be gentle with yourself. If you can, lie down to integrate the process.

Note: Letting go means not being attached to feeling either positive or negative emotions. Observe without judgment, and don't identify with how you feel. Witness your emotions from a space where you can experience them without letting them overwhelm you. The goal is to let go of the attachment, not the emotion.

Emotions are part of our experience of being human. They're important for inspiration, intuition, and for guiding you to who you want to be and what you want to do in life. Difficult emotions, such as anger and fear, have played a key role in keeping us alive. We want to learn to use these emotions to respond in appropriate ways.

4

Your Inner Child

*Once you get to know your inner child, you will understand who
you are in profound and heartfelt detail.*
—Lesley Epperson

The Inner Child carries wounds from early childhood experiences. As a child, you formed beliefs—based on limited
understanding—about what was going on and what it meant.
These beliefs were carried into adulthood by a part of yourself
who was never able to reconcile what happened. Your inner child
is still fighting this battle for you. This child wants and needs to
express itself and be heard, understood, protected, and loved by
you, its adult self.

An inappropriate response or reaction to a trigger can often
represent the inner child asking for healing. When you see repeating patterns in life that make you feel a certain way, these
can lead you to the beliefs held by your inner child. You may not
remember the situation or how you reacted, but you'll find clues
in your relationships, life choices, and behaviors.

Inner-child work can range from simple to complex, depending on what you experienced as a child trying to navigate an adult world. The processes that follow are not an exhaustive approach to working with or healing the inner child. The goal here is simply to provide information valuable in the quest for self-love.

Process 7: The World of Your Inner Child

This is an introduction to the world of your inner child. Create a timeline of any childhood events you remember, ranging anywhere from birth to twenty years. Write down any memories, your approximate age at the time, and a brief description. Include events that had an effect on you. They could be happy, sad, confusing, sudden changes, unexpected wins, anything that rocked your world. This timeline isn't meant to be a complete outline of your childhood. Continue to add to it whenever you remember notable events.

Process 8: Give the Child A Voice

There are options for doing this powerful process. Letter writing, journaling, and conversing with your inner child are commonly used techniques. The goal is to allow your inner child to express their feelings, to know they have the right to feel that way, and to reassure the child within that you're ready to help them understand and heal. These processes can be most effective when you feel upset, which is a signal that your inner child is also upset.

Letter writing

This is a form of automatic writing in which you write without thinking about whatever wants to come up. When you're annoyed or frustrated, it's likely your inner child is feeling the same. You'll need two sheets of paper for this process. You'll also need two large envelopes to keep the letters in, labeled ADULT and CHILD. One is for letters from you to your inner child; the other for letters from your inner child to you. Prior to starting the process, ask your inner child how they're doing. Then start writing.

The first letter is from your inner child to you. Start with whatever version of "Dear Adult Me" you wish to use. Then begin to write a letter from the younger version of you. Don't judge or edit what you're writing, just let the words flow. Write from a child's point of view, where circumstances and events might not have made sense. Write as much or as little as you want for this first letter. You're opening a dialogue between you and your younger self. Let the anger, hurt, pain, grievances, distortions, and confusion come to the surface with no boundaries—you're giving your inner child a voice.

The second letter is from you to your inner child. In the letter you write back, address the letter to you as a child. Again, write without thinking or judging yourself. Acknowledge your inner child's pain and frustration. Under the circumstances, they had a right to feel that way. Reassure them that although you might not have been available in the past, you're here now to protect and love them in the way they always deserved. Thank them for being brave and willing to share. Reassure them that you love them and will be there anytime they need you.

Read the letters before putting them in the envelopes. Let your tears flow or anger rage. This is an emotional process that deserves to be fully felt. To be most effective, letter writing should be done any time you feel upset, so your inner child learns to trust you will be there for them.

Journaling

Journaling allows you to gain insights into the world of your inner child by exploring the world they inhabit. You begin to understand—through emotions, experiences, and memories—what the world was like for your younger self and how you felt about it. The use of journaling invites you to remember and describe places, events, feelings, favorite activities, and dreams you've forgotten. Unlike the timeline you created of events in your life, this journal should include as many details as you can provide and the way each affected you at the time. Journaling creates a rich tapestry of your history.

Use the following questions as a starting point. Then search for additional, more detailed journaling prompts, or buy an inner-child journal that includes in-depth prompts to deepen your exploration.

Initial Journaling Prompts

- What is your earliest childhood memory? Describe the people around you and where you were. How did you feel?
- What was the most difficult part of childhood for you?
- What was the best part of your childhood?
- Did you feel free to be yourself?

- What did you most like to do as a child?
- Describe the first bedroom you remember.
- What did you worry about? How did you feel about it?
- Is there a treasured memory that you've kept in your heart? Describe what happened and who you were with.
- If you could talk to your younger self, what questions would you ask?

Conversation

Talking to your inner child is a powerful tool for the times when you feel most upset. You can do this right after an event occurs or a few days later, when you're more likely to understand what triggered you or made you react in an excessive way. There are many ways to approach your inner child. You might want to refer back to some of the questions you want to ask your younger self.

To begin the process, imagine you're standing in front of the first house you recall living in as a young child. Open the front door and find your bedroom. As you open the door, you see your inner child sitting on the bed. They recognize you as an older version of them. If you feel comfortable, walk into the room and sit next to them. Tell them you would have come to check on them sooner but didn't know how to reach them.

Ask them how they're doing and let them know how you're feeling. Tell them you think something must have upset them, and let them know it's okay now to express how they feel in whatever way they need to. You understand why they acted in a certain way—to stay safe or hidden, to avoid conflict. You're an adult now, and allowing those feelings to come up is a way for both of you to heal.

Listen for a response, or pretend the child is responding the way you originally wanted to. Let them scream, cry, pound the pillows, whatever helps them release their frustrations. They need to know you understand how they feel. You can tell them anything that would've made you feel better at the time. Promise you'll be back to check on them now that you know how.

Thank your younger self for keeping you safe. Eventually you'll have longer conversations with them, delving deeply into your shared experiences. The goal is to allow your inner child to heal and integrate with the adult you. In the future, you can do this by inviting them to come live with you, showing them where you live and reassuring them you'll protect them from now on. For now, simply give you as a child a long hug.

Process 9: You are Worthy of Love

In this process, imagine you're holding yourself as a baby. If you have difficulty imagining that, cradle a stuffed animal in your arms. Tell yourself everything you wish you'd been told as a child. Things you might say include:

- You are so smart.
- I'm so lucky to have you.
- You're incredibly beautiful.
- You are a special gift.
- You are perfect in every way.
- What a joy it is to take care of you.
- I'll always be here when you need me.

- I love you much more than you know.
- You are so brave and kind.

Do this when your spirits need a lift. Feel the words resonate in your heart. This is a powerful way to reassure yourself that you are and always have been worthy of love.

5

Be Your Best Friend

*Treat yourself like you would your best friend, because
you are the only one who is always there for you.*
—Lesley Epperson

You are the one constant in your life. You are always with you. You can count on you being there. You're the best friend you'll ever have. You'll go through birth and death by yourself, but you're never truly alone.

At times you may treat yourself like an enemy. To transition from enemy to ally is to become your own best friend. We all make mistakes, we struggle, we fail, we face adversity, we overcome, and we start over. With you by your side, you can provide the compassion, forgiveness, hope, and faith you need to carry on.

Speak to yourself as you would to a best friend when you want to make them feel better. Show yourself that you care. Never say anything to yourself that you wouldn't say to a close friend. We can be our own worst critic, judging our every action and blaming ourselves. This is important because there's a difference between *who you think you should be* according to what you've been told, and *who you really are.*

Process 10: Hug Yourself

Touch gives us a sense of comfort, belonging, and security. Research tells us we need at least eight hugs a day. If you're lacking physical touch, try one of these ways to hug yourself:

- Wrap your arms around yourself and squeeze.
- Curl up with a body pillow or hug a regular pillow.
- Wrap a weighted blanket around yourself for a body hug.
- Cuddle up with and hug your pet.
- Stroke your arms and face lightly to bring back memories of a loved one's touch.
- Remember a treasured hug from a family member, and use your imagination to give and receive that special hug again.
- Give hugs to others whenever you can. Always ask permission first.

Process 11: Build Yourself Up

Write three things you appreciate about yourself on separate sticky notes each day or several times a week. Put them where you'll see them every day. These aren't affirmations, but they do confirm who you are. Examples include:

- I love daydreaming.
- I earned every laugh line on my face.

- I enjoy making others laugh or smile.
- I always look for ways to compliment people.
- I love deep discussions about life.
- I am who I am.
- I love who I am, no matter what.

6

Self-Talk

Whatever words we utter should be chosen with care.
—Buddha

At some point in your past, people spoke to you or to each other in negative ways. It could have been family, friends, teachers, colleagues, a significant other, even random people in passing. As children we tend to integrate these opinions as truth. If you find yourself saying things like "I can't do anything right" or "I'll never fit in," know that those ideas didn't come from you. As a child, you knew you were born to be loved.

As an adult you find yourself making statements similar to what you heard growing up. What you tell yourself also plays a big part in who you are and what you experience. These thoughts can keep you from pursuing a dream or achieving a goal.

You might be an optimistic person, but once you start listening to what you say to yourself on a daily basis, you'll notice that much of it is negative. It's not easy to change negative self-talk, and it's unlikely you can completely eliminate it, but with awareness, time, and patience, you can transform what you tell yourself.

Process 12: Watch Your Words

The words you use when talking to yourself or others matter. Your subconscious mind can't distinguish between the reality of what you say and the reality of what you mean. Its job is to keep you safe at any cost.

When you say something like "This job is killing me" or "They make me sick," your subconscious mind takes your words literally. Since it's focused on keeping you safe, it can't allow you to go on working at a job that you've described as killing you, or let you keep hanging out with people who you've said make you sick. It has no choice but to assume those words are your reality, and it has to get you out of such situations.

If your job is killing you, your mind will start to look for ways to prevent you from dying. It must get you out of that job. If your partner is making you sick, your mind will ensure your safety by ruining the relationship.

Make a list of words you use that have negative connotations. Then change those words. Instead of "My back is killing me" you can say, "I'm experiencing discomfort in my back." Other common phrases people use include:

I am lonely.	I have lots of friends who care.
No one likes me.	All the people who know me love me.
My job is a nightmare.	This job pays me, so I can follow my dreams.

Highlight the word or words you want to change in your conversations, especially in conversations with yourself. Then, in Process 13, use what you've learned to transform what you say to yourself.

7

———————

Create New Beliefs

What we speak becomes the house we live in.
—Hafiz

Thoughts matter. What you think affects how you feel about yourself. Notice the difference in how you feel when you think I *may not always get it right, but I'm working on it* instead of *That was a stupid thing to do.* That's not letting yourself off the hook—that's being human.

Repeated thoughts—positive or negative—become ingrained in your subconscious mind. Everyone has negative thought patterns. The first step in creating new beliefs is to become aware of the old ones. Too often, by the time you notice what you're unconsciously saying to yourself, those thoughts have become beliefs.

In order to genuinely love yourself you need to consider what you say to yourself every day. Once you begin to recognize your negative voice, you can start speaking to yourself in a positive way. Change your thoughts to change your mind and transform your story.

Process 13: Transform What You Say to Yourself

When you hear yourself say things like "No one cares about me" or "No one loves me," you're telling yourself you don't matter. You can change these into "There are many people who care about me" and "I am loved by everyone who knows me—and I know me best." Reverse what you're saying to yourself and add words that emphasize how you want to feel. Keep a list of what you say to yourself and how you transform it into a positive statement. Post the list where you can see and update it.

Positive self-talk can lead to improved self-esteem, greater vitality, and increased satisfaction with life. Over time, it will change how you feel about yourself and the world you live in.

Process 14: Affirmations Create New Beliefs

Beliefs are thoughts repeated many times. Affirmations can create new beliefs when you repeat them often, one of the reasons they're so effective. When you say an affirmation, your subconscious mind doesn't know it's not the current situation. Repeating affirmations makes them appear true to the subconscious.

There are some rules around composing affirmations. They should be in present tense and use action verbs. Include any words that bring up strong emotions for you. To own these statements, preface them with "I claim" or "I know." You can end with "or better" to ensure they're flexible. Here are some examples of powerful affirmations:

- I am more than enough.
- I believe in myself.

- I am worthy of all I desire, or better.
- I am gentle and kind to myself.
- I am happy, healthy, wealthy, and blessed.
- I love all the ways that I am unique.
- I speak to myself with compassion and understanding.
- I am grateful for how each day unfolds.
- I love all of me, including the flaws and desires that make me human.
- An abundance of love and prosperity surrounds me.
- I belong here and have much to offer the world.

Create ten affirmations that resonate with you, and write them down. For a week, state these affirmations aloud and with feeling every morning and night. You may want to add them to your journal, as writing them down makes them more powerful. Continue to repeat these affirmations until you believe them. Don't worry if you can't come up with ten at first. You can always modify or add to your list until you have ten you genuinely believe.

8

Courage to Be You

To be yourself in a world that is constantly trying to make you something else is the greatest achievement.
—Ralph Waldo Emerson

It takes courage to let the world know the real you. When you wear a mask, you act in ways you think will make you fit in. To be authentic is to step out from behind the mask and express who you really are, no matter how scary it might be. It can be terrifying if you were raised in a family that didn't express emotions or value your opinions, or if you were punished for saying what you thought. Let go of those memories and embrace the desire to be yourself.

Courage allows you to be vulnerable and express your views honestly while having the presence to truly listen to those around you. Beyond expressing yourself, authenticity is knowing who you are and what values you hold, and making decisions that align with those values. It's also the freedom to redefine your beliefs, follow your dreams, and live the life you desire.

To do this, you must possess unshakable respect for yourself and others. Trust that your opinions and actions are consistent with your values. Understand that we are all unique. Be considerate and thoughtful when others disagree with you.

A big step toward cultivating self-love is unveiling yourself to yourself. Appreciate all that you are and accept what you wish to change. Accept that other people's values and actions will differ from yours when they too are authentic. Listen with presence, curiosity, and interest when you're engaged in an honest conversation.

Process 15: Values and Beliefs

Make a list of the characteristics you value most, what inspires you, and what keeps you up at night. These can include what you admire about yourself or others. For each, identify a belief you hold about it. If the belief is negative or vague, rewrite it to match what you want to believe. You'll have three columns: VALUE, CURRENT BELIEF, NEW BELIEF.

Values help you discover who you really are and who you want to be. Beliefs let you integrate these values into your life. Positive beliefs allow you to reframe your thoughts to better align with your highest values.

Process 16: Authentic Communication

Think of a friend you'd like to have a heart-to-heart conversation with. Write down a few sentences you'd like to say to them. Remember, what you say should reflect your values, be communicated with complete trust in yourself and your opinions, and be genuine. Allow yourself to be as vulnerable as you can.

Practice speaking the sentences aloud. Note the tone of your voice. Thoughts may come up randomly. Express them. Don't worry about memorizing or writing them down. In a real conversation, what each person says will change the course of the conversation. Since you're learning how to communicate and listen in more thoughtful and encouraging ways, the words will eventually come naturally. Stay positive and engaged in the interaction, gently agree to disagree, and be focused and attentive throughout.

This is practice, not a script. With time and practice, you'll learn from mistakes and become more comfortable with revealing your true self. Be patient as you let more of your feelings, fears, and desires come forward.

It's possible that the person you're talking to might become defensive or angry. Don't react. Gently guide them back to the conversation with compassion and encouragement. If all else fails, you can let them know that maybe this isn't the best time to talk, that what you'd like to discuss can wait.

9

Lucky To Be You

Be yourself; everyone else is already taken.
—Oscar Wilde

Celebrate who you are and who you'll become in life. Acknowledge and honor yourself daily for all you've learned and overcome. Be proud of your accomplishments. Give yourself a high five. Put on your favorite playlist and sing and dance like no one's watching. Make yourself laugh with a joke only you understand.

Embrace all your talents, gifts, struggles, and flaws.
The successes and failures, wins, losses, and draws.
A smile for a stranger, the words that you speak.
Together these make who you are quite unique.
You are lucky to be here. You have made it so far.
When you love yourself, you can be who you are.
—Lesley Epperson

Process 17: It's Enjoy-Yourself Day!

Wear something that reflects who you are in a unique way. Be relaxed and curious. Do something out of the ordinary. Take yourself to a concert, a new restaurant, window shopping, or sit on a bench and watch the sunset. Spend time in nature. Find a free poetry reading or art opening. You don't have to spend a lot of money or do anything fancy. Just spend the day with yourself.

Be present in the moment, doing something you rarely allow yourself to do. It's time to celebrate yourself. Life isn't easy, but you can delight in small miracles and the great beauty each day brings. Smile. Dance down the sidewalk or in your chair. Laugh. Ask questions. Explore who you are.

Always be grateful for the unique and remarkable person you are.

10

It Happens One Day

To love oneself is the beginning of a life-long romance.
—Oscar Wilde

One day you'll be following your normal routine and something will happen. It could be when you tell yourself "I love you" and feel your heart smile. You may think *This isn't a big deal.* You've sensed it growing. It's good to know you *can* love yourself. And that is a very big deal.

This isn't the end of the journey. The seed of self-love is blossoming inside you. A seed you planted and watered and nurtured. It's ready for sunshine and fresh air. It's the warmth of spring that surprises you in the middle of winter. It's a peek at what is possible.

There's no way to explain the feeling, knowing it's possible. You'll understand when it happens. Once you accept the fact that self-love is available to you, the tenderness and compassion and love for who you are will continue to grow. It will flow from your heart to other hearts, from conditional to unconditional love for yourself and for others.

This doesn't happen quickly or without heroic effort, but loving yourself without criticism or judgment is worth the dedication it takes every day. Without loving yourself, you can't show others how to love you. Only when you love yourself will you see that love reflected in the eyes of another.

This is the beginning of the self-love journey. It takes patience and understanding and the willingness to go deep inside yourself, forgive yourself, know who you are, and accept all of you. Then you can experience life from the perspective of knowing you're worth it, every moment and every day. At its core, self-love is fundamental to living the life of your dreams. Dream big!

Process 18: Surrounded by Love

Choose statements that resonate with you and write them on sticky notes. Put the notes where you'll see them often. Use words you wish you'd heard as a child. By repeating these affirmations—aloud and with feeling—you're creating the future you desire. You are surrounding yourself with love.

Examples you can use include:

- I love who I am.
- I love every part of me.
- I listen to and honor myself.
- I treat myself with compassion and understanding.
- I forgive myself, for myself.
- I am grateful for who I am.
- I matter greatly to many.
- I am important because I exist.

- I am special and gifted.
- I am unique and extremely talented.
- I am always loved.
- Love comes to me easily and effortlessly.

11

Navigating Change

*It is our attitude at the beginning of a difficult task which,
more than anything else, will affect its successful outcome.*
—William James

Change is part of life. You will face challenges that test whether you accept and embrace—or reject—an opportunity for growth. The waves of change won't shake you to the core if you go with the flow. You've been through it all many times before. Step back and take stock. You can handle anything when you understand what needs to be done.

Facing multiple challenges at once can be overwhelming unless you're prepared to conquer them. Reframe the situation and face it with balance and grace. Ask yourself, "What is the worst that could happen?" Your ego is telling you it's a catastrophe, and if you believe that, it could be.

Remember the times you dealt with adversity in the past. How did you do it? How did you feel when you overcame a difficult situation? Did you feel stronger and more resilient? What lessons did you learn?

Challenging times become easier once you identify how life is asking you to expand and grow. When you're going through overwhelming situations, baby steps are better than great leaps. To find clarity, ask yourself the following questions:

- What steps do I need to follow to get through this?
- What are the most important steps I need to take?
- What's standing between me and completion?
- What am I afraid of?

You are more prepared to succeed than you've ever been. You've got this!

Process 19: Organize Life

Write down the challenges you're facing. Also include the responsibilities you take on every day. Assign each a priority from 1 to 5 and group them by priority, giving the most important items a 1, the least important a 5.

For each challenge, list what needs to be done. Some items won't need any additional action. These could be your normal responsibilities, or things that are out of your control. Also consider anyone who might be able to help you.

For new challenges, write down who, what, where, when, and how for each. These might not be as big as your mind is making them out to be. If you have a trusted friend, discuss how overwhelmed you feel and ask for any ideas about how to deal with it. Listen to your friend. Take notes if you need to.

Ask yourself:
- Does this have to be done by me? Am I the only one who can do it?
- Is there someone who can help me? Can I delegate any tasks to someone I trust?
- Does it have to be done the way I would do it, or is there a better way?
- Is there a solution to this problem that I haven't considered?
- Can the bigger issues be broken down into smaller steps?
- Why is it causing me so much worry and stress?
- What is the worst that can happen?

Use a calendar to add your normal responsibilities to the days they need to be done. Then add the new items that you need to manage. Add no more than one or two new steps to each date. Put things in perspective. It's important to make sure you handle your responsibilities to yourself and others. Most challenges you'll face are temporary and unlikely to continue.

If you have trouble coming up with a solution for a particularly difficult item, break it down into manageable steps and add those to the calendar. In order to gain control of your time, make sure to list smaller steps in logical order and put no more than two or three on any one date.

Even though your calendar is full, you now have an estimated end date. You have an action plan. Life will happen. Things will change. Keep the calendar handy to see what you need to do each day. Using an online calendar makes it easy to move things around. If you can't take care of something one day, move it to the next. Then take a step back and see if it's doable.

Breathe. Quiet your busy mind. Give yourself a hug. Know that this challenge will end and that you'll understand why it happened. Congratulate yourself for making sense out of chaos. Express gratitude to life for the opportunity to gain insight into yourself and develop the strength to face difficult times.

12

Tending the Garden

Plant a Seed so your Heart will Grow.
—Hafiz

Self-love requires careful tending, much like a garden. During tough times, weeds appear and grass creeps in. The carefully planted garden may be overrun with bugs and spiders. Plants need to be harvested and flowers cut for a garden to stay healthy. You prune and water and feed. You watch your garden grow.

When life's challenges demand more of your time and attention, it's easy to forget to tend your inner garden. To maintain the garden of self-love in the midst of life is no easy task. By thinking of self-love as a garden, we plan, prepare, plant, and nurture; we remember the steps we've taken to get to the harvest. It might not be unconditional, but we know that we love and appreciate who we are. The nourishing bounty of self-love is worth the work.

Process 20: Growing Self-Love

You prepare the soil and decide what you want to plant. This is when you begin to think about self-love and discover whether you genuinely love yourself or not. This can take time as you wind your way through what you feel, deciding whether you want to plant a garden and, if so, what you want to grow. During the planning stage, you'll uncover why you want to make the investment in self-love.

Once the soil is ready, you plant the seeds. At this stage, you tell yourself "I love you" no matter how far from reality it seems. When you plant seeds in your garden, you have faith that they'll sprout from the soil and grow into what you expect them to be. Your faith leads you from not knowing whether you'll be able to love yourself to the whisper of hope when it breaks through the soil.

No matter how much faith you have in the garden's potential, seeds can't grow without water. You have to heal emotions that stand in the way of seedlings seeking the sun. You remove anything that blocks them from reaching the surface, as the sunshine warms the soil and coaxes sprouts to break through. Never give up on what doesn't appear right away. Loving yourself takes time and effort, but the harvest will be worth it.

No matter how carefully you plant the seeds, water shifts the soil and seedlings move. When you learn how to express your emotions, you'll shift into a new phase, and from this space you will continue the journey to self-love. Watch the new plants grow and thin as needed, checking daily for an overcrowded garden. As emotions continue to come up to be healed, take time to address them before they become inextricably intertwined and difficult to remove.

It's easier to maintain the garden daily than to wait until harvest. Plants need loving attention, as does your inner child when you recognize an inappropriate response. Listen to the child within and watch yourself thrive as you give them the attention required to heal wounds buried deep in the past. Caring for your inner garden is crucial to ensure a great bounty.

As the plants begin to stand on their own, it's time to fertilize and mulch to encourage growth and discourage pests. The food and mulch must be right for each stage of growth. You don't want to burn the young plants with the wrong nutrients or bury them under mulch that's too thick. When you're careful how you treat yourself, you nurture the relationship between your inner and outer aspects. You are your own best friend.

Now you can sit back in a shady spot and watch your garden grow. You feel the beginnings of love for yourself as you continue to water and feed your soul. The sun and soil do much of the work, reflecting how much you've invested in yourself and in your garden plot. Celebrate how far both you and your garden have come, but don't forget to nourish the growth you see in your life. You still need to care for the plants and for you.

One day you notice weeds sprouting alongside your plants. Remove any as they pop up, and check your plants for pests. They don't wait until harvest to eat. If you notice that negative self-talk has crept back in, pull it up by the roots. Some plants may develop stray branches and need to be pruned. As you cut away old beliefs that no longer serve you, you make space for new beliefs.

Negative thinking has an insidious way of coming back when you focus on other tasks, and your mind is more than happy to go back to weed-infested and uncomfortable thoughts. Remove the weeds and prune the plants. Caring for plants, touching them, talking to them, is nurturing for the garden. It takes effort to rid your mental garden of negative thoughts, and self-care helps mend those places where they sneak in.

Bugs and pests are the bane of the garden. They make your fresh new forest of green their new home, and eat the leaves that gather energy needed for plants to bloom, snacking on roots until a plant wilts or dies. Finding them on your plants is nowhere near as challenging as making them move on to less well-tended gardens.

Look for safe alternatives to chemicals, and devise a plan to conquer this microcosmic challenge. Treating bugs and other garden pests naturally leads to healthier plants, soil, and people. It can be overwhelming, but once you identify which pests are munching your plants you can find ways to relocate them. Everyone has thoughts and feelings that ambush and trap them or nibble away at their spirit. Investigate where those thoughts came from and free yourself of mental pests through awareness and self-care.

In the end, you'll forget all the aches and pains, all the work it took to get here. Your garden is filled with enough to share with friends and family. Embrace the miracle: a tiny seed grows into a plant with blossoms, the wonder of a bloom that transforms into a fruit or vegetable, the heart-warming beauty of flowers on the table. Enjoy the simple act of letting self-love continue to grow and thrive. Who knows what the blooms in your heart may bring, all because you set out on a journey to love yourself and to love yourself more.

13

—————————

Affirmations

Affirmations should be in present tense, use action verbs, and reflect what you desire in a positive way. They're more powerful when they include emotionally charged words such as incredibly, awesome, joyfully, happy, satisfied, confidently, and greatly.

Affirmations

I am always loved.
I am loving and in this I am loved.
I love who I am.
I love all parts of me.
I accept what is and let go of what isn't.
I listen to and honor myself.
I'm grateful for who I am and who I'm becoming.
I see every challenge as an opportunity to learn.

Affirmations With Emotional Words Added

I am always greatly loved.
I am joyfully loving and in this I am loved.
I am truly blessed and excited to love who I am.
I embrace and love all parts of the incredible me.
I am satisfied to accept what is and let go of what isn't.
I confidently listen to and honor my magnificent self.
I am eternally grateful for who I am and who I'm becoming.
I welcome challenges as an opportunity to love myself more.

These affirmations are meant to get you started. There are lots of sources of information about affirmations. Books, journals, and websites include affirmations and quotes you can use for inspiration. Create your own once you understand how to put together powerful affirmations that don't rely on other people or on specific outcomes, which can diminish their effectiveness.

14

Enlist Help When You Need It

There are times when you'll feel confused and overwhelmed by life. Whether you need to process feelings, thoughts, or insights, it's best to have an experienced professional by your side. It can take time to find the right therapist or counselor and to develop a trusting relationship. Trust that you'll know when you connect with the right person.

I recommend working with a therapist when doing emotional clearing, inner-child work, and shadow work. They have the tools and knowledge to guide you through what can be tumultuous and emotionally demanding. Though your friends and family might be willing to listen, it's better to find someone who's professionally trained to help you navigate tough times. You can spare yourself from misguided advice and save your relationships from burnout.

One common therapy, cognitive behavior therapy (CBT), is a widespread practice area whose goal is to help people develop better coping skills to identify and change any problematic thoughts, feelings, and behaviors.

Another popular therapy is Emotional Freedom Technique (EFT), which uses tapping on a series of acupuncture points on the body while repeating a statement about the issue you're tapping on. This helps interrupt intrusive thoughts and feelings and calm them. A great deal of information about tapping is available on the internet.

Regardless of specialization, a therapist or counselor will be able to work with you to redirect and reframe your thoughts. Listen to your intuition before committing to work long-term with a specific therapist or counselor. Interview more than one to find the person who best meets your needs.

Resources

Books

The following books provide a far deeper dive into certain processes than I've presented here. These are books I consulted when I felt ready to learn more.

Gawain, Shakti. *Creative Visualization*. Bantam Books, NY, NY (1979, 1982).

Jackman, Robert, LCPC. *Healing Your Lost Inner Child*. Practical Wisdom Press, United States (2020).

Ruskan, John. *Deep Clearing*. R. Wyler & Co., New York, NY (2001).

Additional Resources

John Newton and Ancestral Clearing
(http://www.healthbeyondbelief.com)

Ancestral Clearing practice for releasing the past through powerful forgiveness prayers. John offers a free call around the first Saturday of the month. Check the website for schedule.

Marisa Peer and Rapid Transformational Therapy
(https://marisapeer.com)

Marisa Peer is a best-selling author, creator of the Rapid Transformational therapy (RTT) technique, and started the I Am Enough movement. The hypnosis and psychotherapy techniques she has developed are powerful and highly effective. Find Marisa's videos on her YouTube channel and website, including many on self-love and healing the inner child.

Sacred Spaces

Create a sacred space in which to meditate or do emotional clearing and inner-child work. It can be a shelf with a favorite picture of you as a child, cherished books, and journals. It can be a table for fresh flowers, plants, and candles. It can be a bench under a tree in the backyard. Creating your sacred space can provide comfort, privacy, and a helpful place to reflect.

Sounds

You can find an array of guided meditations, frequency music, mantras, and sound baths on the internet. These can be deeply calming, even played at low volume. YouTube has enough options to find the ones that speak to you. You can also use chimes, gongs, or your voice to make your own sounds.

About the Author

Lesley Epperson has been reading, writing, playing music, and asking questions since the age of five. Born and raised in Texas, she moved west at the urging of Angels who said, "Go to California and write a book." She lives a simple life on the Northern California coast, where the Pacific Ocean and her trusty companion Juju demand ocean walks and meditations to calm the soul. Lesley loves hiking in the redwoods, exploring the coastal cliffs, rock hunting, and going on magical adventures.

Lesley Epperson is also a transformational life coach specializing in self-discovery and trauma recovery. She continues to question the nature of reality.